GATHERING FLOWERS OF THE MIND:

COLLECTED POEMS 1996 - 2020

Writing by the same author

www.theburningarchive.com

GATHERING FLOWERS OF THE MIND:

COLLECTED POEMS

1996 - 2020

Jeff Rich

Burning Archive Press

Melbourne

Published in 2021

by Burning Archive Press

Copyright © Jeff Rich 2021

Printed in Australia by Ingram Spark

All rights reserved

ISBN 978-0-6451592-0-2

Contents

Preface	I
Part One - Dreams Before The Pills	1
Dream In Terza Rima	3
Exuberance At Last	4
Birth	5
Dream Life	6
Chant	8
Wisteria	10
Lesson In Mirrors	11
Stubby	13
Word Slum	14
I Dreamt	15
Pretence	16
Sunday Afternoon	18
Black Dogs	20
Plain Song	21
Yearning	23
Five Tercets	24
Part Two - After The Pills	25
The Book Of My Soul	27
Axel's Castle	28
Gould's Humming	30
Song	31
Avatar Rains	32
Self Belief	33
The Afternoon Jog	34
Simple Steps	36
A Poet's Burden	37
Not Getting Things Done	38
Gathering	40

Money	42
To My Errant Mind	44
A Gamer's Sonnet	45
Borderlands	46
Poem 99	48
Pale Dissent	49
To Run Again	50
Sanity	51
Dream Less Nights	52
South Ward	53
After The Pills	54
Part Three - The Burning Archive	57
The Burning Archive - The Beginning	59
Time Song	60
Nouriel's Shoes	61
The State Of Politics	63
Timbuktu	65
Power	67
History	68
The Cruel Season	69
Seals Of Silence	70
Prayer	71
Forgotten Stories	72
Lament	73
Kaddish	75
Faith	76
Last Post	77
Seam	79
The Burning Archive	80
No Fixed Position	84
Data	85
Invitation	86
Money Free	87
After Shelley	88

Sunday Morning	89
Weekend Footy	90
The Chinese Ancients	91
Difficulty	92
Re Canto	93
Long Habits	94
The Forest	95
Belated	96
Ode To Coffee	97
The Unwritten Book	98
Monday Morning	99
Skiving Off	100
The Burning Archive - The End	101
Part Four - Dr Cogito's Rebellion	103
Life Expectancy	105
Dr Cogito's Rebellion	106
Dr Cogito's New Job	108
Dr Cogito Admits He Is Mad	109
The Glass Half Full	110
The Exile Of Dr Cogito	111
Dr Cogito's Mission	112
Public Words	113
Insomnia	114
Dr Cogito's Fall	115
One Thousand Steps	117
No Markers	118
Leucoxolyn	120
Barren Books	121
Unribboned	122
Unrealistic Attempt	123
Hoop Of Rescue	126
The Morning News	127
When The Wind Blows From I Know Not Where	128
Snow Falls On The Suburban Plain	129

The Years Drag On Beyond Measure And Form	130
The World Resembles An Eton Mess	131
The Tethered Mind	132
Dr Cogito At Work	133
Long Summer	134
Executive	135
Dr Cogito Brought His Mind To Heel	136
Rocket Man	138
The Poet In A Time Of Terror	139
Dr Cogito Regrets The Futility Of His Existence	141
Dr Cogito Struggles Against Himself	143
Peaches In A Bowl	144
Elegy	145
A History Of Madness	147
Dr Cogito Enters The Feral City	150
Part Five - Meditations	153
Lightness	155
Heaviness	156
Losing My Direction	157
Ode To Another Nightingale	158
Boundless	159
Falling Into Meaning	161
Count Your Breaths	162
Abandoned	163
Every Twist	164
Emptiness	165
The Monstrosity Of Power	166
No Words Are Coming To Me	167
History	168
Sacred Speech	169
Silence	170
Another Generation	171
Late Spring	172
Friendship	173

Twitter Poem	174
Being Nothing	175
The Breath Of Life	176
The Mind	177
Rain Falls In February	178
Winter Phrases	179
Commuter Train	180
Drumming In My Ear	181
The American News	182
I Fold The Paper	183
The Gardener	184
On Renewal	185
On Power	187
Travel Song	188
The State Historical Museum, Moscow	189
The Laws Of History	190
Stoker	193
Fountain	194
The Prophet In A Box	195
Down Time	197

Preface

Emily Dickinson gathered the flowers of her exquisite mind into forty carefully arranged fascicles, small bundles of handwritten pages bound together by hand-stitched thread. Fascicles referred in the nineteenth century to a bunch of flowers or plants held in a bunch, often as a botanical specimen. It is now a word rarely used except to describe the legacy of Dickinson's mind that was discovered at her death.

Over the last thirty years I have collected my own fascicles of poetry, and here in this collection of poems written from the mid 1990s until January 2020, to the cusp of the pandemic and the Great Seclusion, are five fascicles, which I planned, after much prevarication and pondering, to publish separately, but decided ultimately to gather together into this single volume, *Gathering the Flowers of the Mind: Collected Poems 1996-2020*.

Publishing my poetry is a decision I made with some difficulty and late in life. Few of these poems were written with much expectation of publication, and rather they remain for me transcriptions of my experience of creating them. I do not revise with a theory of poetics or a melodrama of perfectionism in my mind. My mental world is altogether too frail and too influenced by Zen aesthetics of *wabi* to revise these poems to death.

Yet I have only slowly shaken off both the fears of rejection by publishers and the mesmerising model of Emily Dickinson's secluded heritage discovered after her death. I have long lived apart from literary and publishing circles, pursuing a modest career as a lowly under-castellan in a minor provincial government, which has induced institutional and legal discouragement to sharing my true voice (if my poems could be said to be that) in the public domain. The quavers and longings in that voice, moreover, have grown less fashionable over the decades, less conforming with the regimented assertions of selected identities, not *différance*, so popular in cultural circles today. Nor did I ever have the entrepreneurial spirit and *chutzpah* to sell my lyrics to whatever market could bear them. I have sheltered from, and not sought out the literary world.

The liberation of authors from commercial publishers, brought on by the internet and technological changes of indie publishing, however, slowly led me to share more of my work with the world. The first of my poems to be published ("Dream Life") appeared in the small journal, *ars poetica*, in 1997. I shared a few poems on online forums, but it was not until 2013 that I came out as a poet, so to speak, and published a selection, *After the Pills*, as an e-book on *smashwords*. Whether a single person has purchased this e-book, other than myself, I do not know. Yet the very act of publishing freely in my own name set me on a new path. Since 2015 I have gathered my poetry, essays and other flowers of my mind at my blog, www.theburningarchive.com. There I have accumulated an online collection of writings on culture, history, literature, madness, memory, psyche and governing, and become less self-concealing as an author. *After the Pills* was a crucial step in that journey. At the age of 50, I finally revealed to the world, in my own name, the writing that was of most meaning to me, that I had been creating despite the weaknesses of my mind for thirty years.

The poems in *After the Pills* were written from the mid-1990s to approximately 2010. They are presented here, with few small revisions to the texts, as the two first fascicles of this collection - *Dreams before the Pills*, and *After the Pills*. The third fascicle, *The Burning Archive*, reflects the title of my blog that was inspired by the series of poems I had been writing since 2010 in the lead up to the inception of the blog, amidst a profound personal crisis in 2015. *Dr Cogito's Rebellion*, my fourth fascicle, contains many of the poems written during, and in the wake of, that period in the wilderness that lasted two to three years, rather than forty days. The title alludes to my reworking of the persona of Mr Cogito created by the great twentieth-century Polish poet, Zbigniew Herbert. Finally, *Meditations* gathers poems from the calmer, more confident, and more reflective two years up to the era of coronavirus.

This collection gathers most of my poetry up until the year of the pandemic. It is not a final collection, or, at least, it is not intended to be. I have in the works other volumes of both poetry and prose that will take less time to bring to the world. While fame is not my spur, fear is now less of a bridle, and honour for the testimony displayed here keeps me riding on. After all, we all have little time to give that testimony, and many ways to join the infinite conversation our ancestors once knew as literature. Whether these poems survive in the culture beyond the moment of their birth, I do not and cannot know. I can only repeat stubbornly Zbigniew Herbert's great words from *The Envoy of Mr Cogito*:

> *go for only thus will you be admitted to the*
>   *company of cold skulls*
> *to the company of your forefathers:*
>   *Gilgamesh Hector Roland*
> *the defenders of the kingdom without bounds*
>   *and the city of ashes*
>
> *Be faithful Go*

Melbourne 2021

PART ONE

DREAMS BEFORE THE PILLS
1996-2006

DREAM IN TERZA RIMA

he wants to say some things about dreams
some things that divide him in images
which play where he cannot act free

forlorn nights without dreams
where he marches lost troopers through the day
anticipating beheaded certainties

arrange and cut and then display
a writer is driven mad in his words
like dreams to condense and displace

he forgets the meanings of words
which have become not sounds but texts
which live now only through encyclopaedias

words stir rebels against life a pretext
to dream of derrida as the homeless one
and antonin making meaning a paranoia

you are divine unreadable or does he mean
incomprehensible that cannot be packaged
inside a page outside a session

EXUBERANCE AT LAST

It's taken me this long - how long?
Thirty-two years eight months and twenty-five
    days
Just to enjoy rhyming impervious.
Warm in bed with my words and my books
I find I like I.
Who cares anyhow about the receiver
(If I keep doing this I'll be broke since
we all know it doesn't pay!).
All we scribblers want fame and luxury of
    meaning,
But the sour critics, the bitter and jealous editors,
the petty journalists dressed up as reviewers -
we all know who they are -
they want to bring us down to share
their gut ache. Thanks Friedrich!
Now but, the words just sing.
Time the Avenger
slips away
and those academic judges leave my room
to dispute Derrida together alone.
Sure I ain't read that much poetry;
I've never done drugs so I'll never make it
as a grunge artist;
I can't even rehearse my forms that well.
Do I even have an ear for what it is that you say?
But I am clever enough to do this.
I enjoy this enough to do this.
What more did Emily need than
those piles unpublished in her room
and daily to cross words with soul?

BIRTH

When you gave separate life to my child,
And her face emerged from long endured pains,
Starting the limp fall of her unmannered
Body into those strong welcoming hands,
I held back a moment, weight on my knee,
And suddenly felt the cold after hours
In your service. Yes - a daughter. Could we
Have imagined how her eyes opened? Our
Intimacy was absolutely free:
Nakedly we kissed before the midwives
And touched her with a finger as if we
Blessed whatever life takes and gives.
While soon the measuring began, shaking,
we held the surging dream of new being.

DREAM LIFE

I

In that small moment dream takes
to fly from memory and become
the nagging image of forgetfulness
the muted clank of psyche's hold
I can turn too well in bed
and learn the pains of comfort.

II

Whenever these rivers of the night
dry hard into red scorched beds
Depression takes over my daily self
like the avenging angel of time.
Scouring winds rub out the image
leaving behind the carcass of summer.

III

Suppose thought gave way to dream.
bridges would collapse. Our simple talk
would become a spree of metaphor
not even poets could afford.
Self would reign over all meaning
and again the tower would fall.

IV

But why do these solitary creations
reveal their meaning first to others
as if the dreaming tongue betrayed
its beloved solipsism? Eyes wrapped
in fabrics of truth and lies,
the dream asks its interlocutor: who?

V

A tree springs from my stomach.
Nebuchadnezzar's madness overcomes time and
    reason
to plant itself in my soil
to come alive again as if
all history is compressed by night
into an image none can forget.

VI

This drowning boat, this fish river,
this Medusa returning as a bowl
of squirming snakes which I eat:
these dreams lie like abandoned gifts
but still share their secret being
with listeners to my night's echo.

CHANT

Every word is denied
Every act is defeated
Every thought is
in error.

We are beaten masks
In search of a theatre and a rite
to give us
voices.

Our culture is dead
And cannot once more be
borrowed into freshness.
Words lie about me
like discarded slogans,
and, in the distance,
the archive burns
while the angel of history
in flight from the arson
turns her face from
her abandoned love.

Soldiers approach me
in Axel's last tower,
isolated
but for these broken books of magic.

I wait to be marched over
composing without
the satisfaction of an audience
the security of a library

worshipping forgotten gods
who die with me
and show the final weakness of art.

"All writing is pig shit"
Now the angel visits
only in dreams.

Every word is denied
Every act is defeated
Every thought is

in error.

WISTERIA

This time of year wisteria
appears from behind the fences
its strangling roots have held tight,
beneath which its clutching roots, hidden all year,
decide at last to reveal its purple grapes
to every passerby
even in this place of concrete.
Some friends of mine held a wisteria party
to celebrate the first full bloom in fifteen years.
Are these months cruel?
Or are these flowers spreading on their vine
without thinking too much?

LESSON IN MIRRORS

I stare at the mirror
relishing how in three weeks
I could forget how to knot my tie.

I have consigned
no fleshless names to nothing
in these three weeks

I have returned to one
though the breath still
hisses across my taut nostril

I have resumed the supreme fiction
and its harsh measures
condemn this delicate silk dress

I have invented to meet
with bosses and colleagues at lunches
full of red wine and cream sauces.

My hands let the tie drop
and it swings a beat
across my tightening chest.

Can these fingers
remember how to weave
a little cloth into a smooth noose?

Or has that voice box
been freed from formal ties
and wants to shoot the breeze?

The lapsed moment ends
when technique finds its breath
to style my eyes after my suit.

STUBBY

The empty bottle sits there
crowning its coaster
accusing me: addict.
Its glass has lost its friendly chill.
The froth has deflated
leaving only a white scum like
detergent washed from a rushing river.
Through its rude transparency
I see the weak yellow liquid
(there's always about a teaspoon left)
sitting dead and stale
of no use to anyone
except me, for this perception.
Across on the shelf
in front of those books
I keep meaning to get to
I spot another one, green this time.
And a brownie with its plain label
half peeled off. And a long thin one,
a lemon wedge drying in its stem
like a boat marooned on air.
What do my neighbours do with their glass?
Sometimes I am the only one who
fills their hessian bag, sometimes two,
each week. They fill the kitchen so quick too
these little glass soldiers
lined up on the window sill
rinsed of their incriminating smell
turned into clean dishes.

WORD SLUM

This Sunday morning my hands smell of bleach
As I stare at this screen hoping words will return
From the place my work has chased them.

Every minute I turn away to listen to my child's
Restless sniffles in the room beside this one -
The writing place, the retreat, the study.

Every surface is strewn with papers, CDs,
Magazines, reports and notes.
It is a word slum.

From this crowded tenement, I must find
In the hour or less I have left
The words who will sing to my woken child.

I DREAMT

I dreamt
I ripped the scab off
Like a band-aid,
Too fast and sharp
To feel any pain.

I dreamt
I suckled from mother's breast
But turned away
When black ink oozed
From her nipples.

I dreamt
I swam down a river
Until its stream became
A pile of gutted fish
On which I slipped when I ran.

Then I dreamt
My house looked on
A golden field of wheat
From which a simple man
With a red barrow, carrying gifts,
Came to visit me.

PRETENCE

Let 's not pretend anymore
That these words matter one jot
Beyond the moment I execute
The deliberated emotion.

No genius outside ordinariness
Haunts me, as I write
Like some rebel ghost
In a line of thinking machines;

The world's fate hangs on another line
Which, I admit, passes through me,
Feeds me and twists me into
Supine gestures;

That we singers and dreamers
Might legislate for the world
Was always the most
Frightening illusion.

Not even performance can raise
These words beyond this *liebstod*, now,
Since all audience has been abolished
By markets and mailing-list sniggers,

And even memory, a shared tongue,
The gentle arpeggios of our history
Are drowned by this bloody
Cacophony of information.
It is silence and absolution
From my own worldliness
That I seek in
These unrepeatable brush strokes.

SUNDAY AFTERNOON

In the hour between packing my child off to a party
And tidying the house for dinner, I imagine a poem.

It is nothing much. I lost faith in my intellect,
Dear neglected instrument, when it left me exposed

Before the burdens of life like a naïve child:
How to make a living, how to raise a child, how to rest at night.

But it is enough. The discipline of couplets puts
Every phrase in a vice, and I can work at it now and then

When the time is there. Nothing more. Nothing less.
A hobby no more dignified or grand than all the other men in sheds

Whittling away at their grandchild's doll.
This simplicity makes me sigh for the lost years

For the drunken years, when in delirium I touched the feet of the tsars
But every morning woke to stale breath and piles of dirty bottles.

All I know now is that the time will end, and
    when she returns,
No doubt tired, wanting food and cuddles, her
    mother exasperated,

This poem will end.
But in the meantime,

Each couplet is short enough that I can keep
    going,
Making meaning, finding joy, going on.

BLACK DOGS

The other night as I lay on my couch for a twisted night of sleep, they howled at me for an hour or more. Poor man who is defeated by these cries, and sits on life like a kitchen stool that wobbles for him. I sit here and watch and wonder if there will ever be a time when these dogs will leave me. That night I sat and thought it's over, it's over, it's over. Middle aged and tired and defeated by money and power and status and class and words and myself and every damn thing in the way. How to go forward here I do not know. Broken man. Shattered poet. He drinks too much. Can any of these words come to anything? I still dream myself as Emily, and that I will be found after death with these piles of unread scribbles. But when the dogs howl I am a suburban dad and official, drawing out a life that goes nowhere that I choose. Can I know any power in any of this? Can I find any way to step from those dogs? Such dead impotence. And even my language has fallen into a dreary tread. No images, just complaints.

PLAIN SONG

Strike the keys like a percussionist.
Push forward even though you know
The days are numbered.

Find the words to sing your songs
Fall away from daily chores and
Office ogres who want everything yesterday.

Now again your song will rise.
In the time, in the habit,
In the tendered garden,

Care will find the spirit.
Quiet will see the dreams.
Routine will find the meaning

These words slip around my ankles like chains.
I find only myself in this encounter
When I hope to find love in words.

I discover that words divide.
They leave me alone in this room,
Cruel and lonely discipline,

But this truth consoles me:
There is no audience
If there is no author.

I scratch at my brain but find nothing
But when I tell a story to my daughter,
Words do flow.

This dumb empty string of lies
Does not help me one bit
It is a torture of depression.

Here on this page
I face meaninglessness.
Where can green hope spring?
No cleverness
No aesthetic
No community

Only dead silent words
Only discovery
My hermitage

Tomorrow I could leave my work life
Like a dirty shirt.
No regrets. No ties.

My skills grow away from my heart.
Fluttering lies for everyone else.
I have begun to live like a shell.

None of this means the least thing.
I have become alien to myself.
I see myself drowning in the ocean.

YEARNING

Day and night, the victims,
Lists of simple words,
Run down my eyes
Falling short of meaning.

Sober nights -
I hit the silence.
Before rest comes,
One question demands conception

But I cannot find it in the lists.
This search...
I was warned!
They saw it coming,
"Thirty-five and a dream of death...
Inexplicable and profound."
Marriage of the mystics.
Blood encircles my feet
While I write in cold night.

Shriven.
In retreat.
No pills will save me
This interrogation.

When will the day end?
When will the question end?
When will the answer fall?
"Yearning makes the heart deep."

FIVE TERCETS

I spend my day in bed when freedom is too hard
The chores that I neglect
Rumbling from behind the door I closed.

These days I cower from the world and know
Myself too weak to fight
The games of power that other men enjoy

Withdraw, I say, withdraw like St Antony,
And find a way beyond
This hedonic mill, this pleasure cruise.

To lacerate your mind, deny your appetite
To bring disaster down
On your head, dream of family deaths in cars

It may be strange liberty, but you fear
Your worst; you fear
Freedom's black mongrel dog at your heel.

PART TWO

AFTER THE PILLS

2006-2012

THE BOOK OF MY SOUL

"The wind bloweth where it listeth, and thou hearest the sound thereof but canst not tell whence it cometh and whither it goeth."
(*John* 3:8).

In a plain bound book
I tattoo white paper in blue
Then wrap myself in this shaman's cloak
To fly with the eagle to a sky renewed.

I sing words salvaged from the press
In the intervals of Te Deum,
Stolen from its church,
Sung so only its melancholy shines.

Pärt turned to church and tradition
Amidst a century of horror
And I turn to these conjured spirits
In a world polluted by podcast trash.

Inwardly, I turn – not without question.
The simplest words are sewn with elaborate
    doubt.
But into the image of inwardness
I dive deeper, and there find reasons to go on.

In the mandalas, strange mazes, of this book
I encircle, tame, and then hold fast
The sound of the blowing wind.

AXEL'S CASTLE

I have always read about Axel's Castle.
Never have I read the work itself.
My work has always been a way to imagine
　　Axel's Castle
Today among sounds of computers and screams
　　of horror.

Castles are things of a broken land
Ruins amidst more modern cities
And in my landscape the only castles
Are commercial fakery for lazy historical fancies.

But the image persists
Through Kafka's obeisant castellans
Bernhard's rants from the lime works
Murnane's cities among the clouds
Sebald's travels through ruins and memory.

Yet to pin this image now precisely,
the way they have done... how?
When I am a homeless drifter
And the castle is the last place
Whence I may declaim against this world
In all its disappointments.

A forest home abandoned to fire.
A beachside shack, whose foundations
Fall into the sea. And in them

A writer abandoned to
his madness and imagination,
Left only with his dirges.

Unclear words:
Refuge of a hermit.

GOULD'S HUMMING

In the first aria he begins to hum.
This is the trace of true art and magic:
Ghostly.
At one with the music but different and beyond.
An *hors-texte* someone might say.
A moment's expression endures through
    recording,
this ghost of the artist,
unbidden, improvised, unscored,
not even beautiful,
but it becomes what I listen for each time:
To search again for traces of the dead in our lives.

SONG

Restless leaves fall from my hands.
My acts flounder and fail.
"Sing to me, sing me out of here,"
My heart yells from a deep hole.
My branches break off in the storm.
While the wind tests my strength,
Threatening to rend me from my home.
One day the wind will overcome me.
One day I will topple, and no longer
Live among the birds striving for the air.
On that day I will fall, and my naked roots
Will stand like skeletons above my ruin.
But till that day I will sing farewell
To each fallen leaf, each storm rent branch.

AVATAR RAINS

It often rains in the Vale.
This place that is no place
But known by millions.
My hunter searches the jungle for a pet:
Tames the named beast;
And hears a chorus of guild grats
For her next level's ding.
In the rain she stands
With an heroic presence;
Otherwise I do not know,
And true affection begins
For this unreal tiger.
While configuring my mods,
The tiger releases a frustrated growl,
Urging me on for more food, more kills.
Then the wizardry of digits
Summons me back from its technicalities
To its true imagined world.

SELF BELIEF

When in an hypnotic state
The suggestion comes:
All these struggles are self-imposed;
One day I will feel at home.

To set aside the nagging doubt,
To write with a fluent hope of reward,
To imagine the vision accomplished and read,
These all seem too real to be true.

Then when the image floats
Slowly and unprompted in a morning of
    headaches
Words break through the dam
Ideas become themselves at last.

The puppet show that plays out in my mind
Can finally find its way to text.
The images that I hold tight and secretly
Release themselves for others to interpret.

Some poetry belongs in schools.
Some texts belong to interpreters.
This small page of words
Once belonged to me.

THE AFTERNOON JOG

At forty-five I still go out for my afternoon jog
Though its time is unreliable
Fitted in between children and chores

These days a dog accompanies me
Knocking off its daily exercise too
While I listen to podcasts about my game

The first few stretches warm you up
By the time I reach the corner shop lights
I am puffing enough to bend over for breath

But I pound away past McDonalds
Down past the Box Hill Hawks oval
Then climb my way slowly up Whitehorse Road

Passing friends of my daughter call out my name
They giggle with her at school
Making imitations of my slow and clumsy style

But the silence of the ipod keeps me safe
From teenage scrutiny
From the mockery of the young

At 40 minutes I feel the pinch
But keep pushing through
By the time I reach home I am spent

I enter the zone about half way
Imagining takes its hold

Stories come to my mind and ride on the euphoric wave.

Fantasies about football.
Plotting about my game.
Conspiracies about my work.

The brain releases itself from its cognitive chains.
It floats to a more restful place.
Relaxed and plastic it becomes free.

My achilles tendons have given me strife
As they are destined to do
But with a physio's help I stay on the track

A graying marathon man
Covering the same old suburban route:
A hero of fitness or a try hard?

This run for freedom for me
Appears to be a crazy old habit to them:
And it is destined to fail one day.

But until that day
It keeps me insane:
The crazy old man of Blackburn.

SIMPLE STEPS

When the mind loiters beyond its rules
Shadowy misery crawls over my skin.
It wraps itself tightly against my bonds,
Holding me more sharply than crowning thorns.

These are the times for simple steps:
One at a time, one after the other.
Find a word here, and spin around its thread
The notions discovered in desert dreams.

Take it down like God's secretary.
Repeat the mantras that have led me
From erring sadness to working quiet;
From worry that garrottes my voice,

To an even plateau, high above the clouds,
Where through thin air
Across flowered fields
I run, left then right, towards a fading sun.

A POET'S BURDEN

Shimmering words.
The moments that I pursue
When life twists unconscionably.

Words that spill without meaning:
Unbidden words, mistakes even.

These moments of pure listening
When all the daily screens fall away
When burden becomes just six letters

Artfully arranged
Signifying nothing

When my broken house of being
Takes in these refugees.

NOT GETTING THINGS DONE

They are evasive – those things
That will not be done.

Like lifting a hero's burden,
Unravelling mysteries,

Forgetting about money, or
Making sense of your super.

They slide from your grasp
Like an eel to be cut.

Politics freed from corruption.
Emotions made into intelligence.

Power's maze escaped.
A mentor's influence overcome.

Secure from life hackers - they slow you down
Like a virus in your boot sector.

They pile in corners,
Messed up, with no priorities,

But asking you each day
To return to their call.

When, after all, will you get around
To relinquishing your youthful strength,

Saying, at last, comfort is attained,
Settling on the meaning of your dreams?

You know you want to spurn productivity,
Refuse luxury, and tarnish beauty's sheen,

But these undone duties
Make their way to daily lists,

Debts demanding payment,
At the bottom of the diary's page.

Heartache untended, dreams undiscovered,
Quests unheeded, pain undressed.

As the day proceeds, more futility is added
to the list for ticking off;

In meticulous notebooks they wait,
Expecting never to be.

Whole careers, projects without plans,
Journeys of recovery and feats of weakness

Pile like chaos in the attic
Awaiting defeat

By distraction and habit and boredom and chance:
Four deadly horsemen more real than the rest.

GATHERING

In dusty corners lie the notebooks I forgot.
This morning I get the vacuum out,
And leaf through these archives.

Some thoughts are preserved like shining jewels.
Others ponder me, disconnected and afraid,
From a time before I began taking my pills.

This space I call my writer's room,
This neglected now, a gatherer's basket.
I take a few hours to remind myself of me.

The pains, the worries, the obsessions with authors
Who I no longer ever read.
I have written so much, tried to publish so little.

I find an old list of someday maybe things to do.
None are done. The motive for them seems lost,
But the idea to record these wishes restores me.

A diary of a difficult year records my transitions
And my limitations. Notes of memories:
"In a bath, at 17, imagining suicide, no friends,
not knowing how to move forward in life."

A folder of old dreams – that still reverberate.
Dreams from twenty years ago – do I keep them?
Unchecked tattslotto tickets.

Hundreds of morning pages written
To unlock the creative spirit.
I throw these out.

A letter not sent to an ex-girlfriend that starts
"Do you know what it is to fear madness?"
Documents concealed in a box for twenty years

Now thrown out, with a casual fling to the floor.
Purged of the neglected work of thirty years
I face the new spring with empty hands.

MONEY

No friend of money - this counter of value -
You set boundaries around my life.
I always come up short - the 200 grand

That would make the difference.
When I should be composing,
I imagine alternatives to earning it -

Tatts tickets loom large.
For years – since I was a kid –
I have fantasized that one day
In the mail
The cheque will arrive.

When I was little I imagined
The letter would tell me
I was a long lost aristocrat from Britain;

My estate was coming back to me,
And all the frustration,
All the limits,
All the self-sacrifice,
Could now be thrown away.

Hard to think at 45:
You have pissed the cash against the wall
In believing this kind of dream.

The reality floors you.
You stagger, unknowing,
Ready to break down.

There will be no relief
From this grind.
The cheque will never come.

This dirty fiction in numbers -
What we earn, save, are worth, plan for –
Ends up ruling you.

Each morning begins with the question
Not how will I live today
But what will I sell?

TO MY ERRANT MIND

Your dreams grow like a twisted gum.

Years were lost
When the market crippled you.

This dusty room is the archive
Of your failed state.

Now you forget little things –
Passwords, names, and faces.

Has the drink flooded the pathways
You once marched through?

Memories of solving equations -
But now you cannot read them.

Still, I light candles before you
Each Sunday.

Cut off from the common dwelling,
Concealed by our books,

We wait together to show
unknown shards of sudden thought.

A GAMER'S SONNET

The avatars were called dream walkers
Who wrought from a technical paradise
This new fallen world, which in terror releases
The baser dreams of men suborned to vice.

This eternal imagined alternative:
Of a life dwelling at one with the forest
Where shamans and spirits and chants outlive
The armed and dangerous, ironclad strategist.

We hold uncertainly both possibilities
In a dance driven by a hidden shaman's drum.
We contain within our spirits hostilities
That break out in our night time delirium.

We walk the earth in both dream and body
To weave dark magic and love within our tragedy.

BORDERLANDS

I read a journalist's quotes
Telling a new theory
That depression is good for you -
At least, good for the species.

All that rumination -
Some scientist on the make
Reckons in his latest piece –
Sets us free.

Most remarkable of all:
They are dogged, the depressed –
He says, this scientist who I ain't met.
They crack through with new ideas.

Well, nice theory, mate:
But you never asked me.
And if persistence is the same as being stuck,
I guess you've got me.

But depression gives me no
Evolutionary advantage for art.
It does not serve this artist's work.
It has cursed me.

Thirty years of wandering now
- lost, not persisting -
In the borderlands
Where reason and his twin fight.

Not knowing which is which
For days at a time.
Forgetting all the great plans
Laid but a fortnight ago.

Eternally disappointed.
Ever distrustful of the latest thought.
Each day of life needing
More simplicity -
A list of simple tasks –
A run, good sleep, small sessions of writing.

Yes, literature and creation
Loom large to keep this life going.

POEM 99

A strange accident of accounting:
This set of words is the one before the ton.

By custom, in cricket, the batsman tenses
Before he pushes to leg for a single
To make the arbitrary, but magical, century.

Whatever possessed me ten or more years ago
To start numbering these works?

Like Emily Dickinson's collected works
But not as prolific, nor profound, nor elliptic.
The origins are forgotten and erased.

Somewhere in my personal archive
A literary editor - if one is ever found - might find
A corrective to this count.

But for now I roll my wrists,
Guide the ball to the gap
Forward of square,
And run comfortably for one.

PALE DISSENT

You stand alone, friendless and cold,
Faltering at times, but steel
Now runs deep and holds my words
Against the inspection of pale

Dissent that rises in my throat
Like a strange unwanted visitor.
No reverberation this time
Just the endless urge to speak.

It's taken twenty-five years
Moving through three failed careers,
Desolation, ten bitter years
Suckled on the bottle.

Revenants of these mistakes
Will not dwell here.

TO RUN AGAIN

I will not be held to this chair,
An ice-pack binding my mortal knee.
I will not conform to the doctor's drill
To exercise free of weight.

I will run again,
Along the streets and through the parks.
I will run again,
Till the first constricted breaths

Discover an easy rhythm.
I will run again,
Slave-dog in tow,
Beating on the hardened path

The signals my feet
Share with this city.
No ban, no scan, no worried concern
Is enough to shackle

Driving legs, bounding home.
My heart is strong enough to race;
So race I will with burning cheeks.
The doctor's words have fallen.

And, yes, I will run again.

SANITY

Long hardened looks beyond the heart
Savage insight before everyday pleading
Tears held back when pain strikes suddenly
A coat held across the lap despite the wearing heat.
Books that lie, neglected, not forgotten
In a summer house's deepest shadows.

DREAM LESS NIGHTS

Sealed in white cotton
Bathed in SSRIs
My nights have forgotten dream.
Notebooks stand at the ready each morning,
Uselessly covered in dust.

Once I filled them remorselessly
With remains of the strange woman,
The snake-haired temptress,
The ashen guardians walking in shadows.
Now, I know only that memories
Fail me each dawn.

Each day, each night
I wait, anticipating irruption.
Each morning I wake to just routine,
More chores, the next piece of reason.
Will the night play dead until I die?
Will the guests of my buried soul
Escape their early grave?
Am I condemned to an artless list?

No. No. And no again.
This blank page
Demands writing.
A rite of sacrifice must begin -
So from this death
Dreams spring again.

SOUTH WARD

The South Ward women are so infinitely polite;
Laughter and forbearance
Outlast the delusions of the mad.
It is not as if they do not respect the patients,
But they dwell every day in frailty.

My mother says she is enjoying herself,
Assessing what is wrong with the other patients.
The nurses carefully advise me:
Assess for yourself whether you feel comfortable
Taking your mother out.

My day soon will fall through this hole:
The great dark gift of the unwell.

AFTER THE PILLS

Mirtazapine changed my life
Though I do not know how it works.
Just think: a mind can be controlled
By the hidden properties of a pill
That oppose the learned habits of that mind.

Before the pills
I would wander city streets
In the sad seasons
Tears in my eyes, despite my suit,
Unable to speak or act.
I only asked - am I mad?
And in the madness of those days
I could never find the *oeuvre*.
I lost months burying myself,
Hiding from the world and touch.

Flickering in my mind was the one sacred task,
Always forestalled, in its niche,
An icon decorated with dust.
This task screamed at me.
It tore at my face.
It shredded every illusion.
It commanded me.
Still, each day I disobeyed.
I froze in misery.

Then the pills came into my life:
Admission to the ill,
Confession of the weak,
Acknowledgement of the insane.

I watched my mind dissemble,
Resemble and remember into differing selves
Through months of side effects:
Fat accumulated;
My skin darkened with the sun;
Sex was extinguished since
Sleep overcame me early each night;
But the frozen misery receded.

So a blessed thaw arrived in my forties.
Each Sunday, the task was performed.
Voice sprang into the world, line by line.
No more wrangling of meaning into silence.
The regrets do not poison the new spring.
But this fickle mind would never again
Claim sovereignty.

If only twenty years before, I had known the pills:
What might have been?
But my mind has become a courteous stranger.
It is a shifting chemical lake
That I swim through
sometimes with caution,
sometimes with abandon.

After the pills,
Its tides and dreams seem rarer;
But age, rush and business flatten
The peaks and troughs of madness.

The *winterreise* sings of my lost mind:
I sing of my lost love like the hurdy-gurdy man.

PART THREE

THE BURNING ARCHIVE

2012-2016

THE BURNING ARCHIVE - THE BEGINNING

At last the Grand Inquisitor said:
Let the archives burn.

The paper of history weighs us down.
Virtual memory will be the way from now.

A solitary voice rose in protest:
With our memories burn our hearts.

The Inquisitor acted fast:
He unleashed fires, controlled and savage,

Beneath the store houses,
Threw Molotov cocktails in libraries.

A billion pages of etched life
In minutes, memos, letters -

The familiar writing of everyday,
Few metaphors, many more lists.

Within a day, ten thousand years,
And more, gone, gone, gone.

The cord that held us to them,
A line of white ashen hearts.

TIME SONG

The day can disappoint the night's best hopes.
The runner can overwhelm his heart.
A lemon tree, infected with gall wasp, can nourish
 hope.
And a broken chair, left out in the rain, can speak of
 tragedy.

When no words come to the silent soul
When fear erases the neural circuits
When each day seems another hopeless sally to a
 killing field
Then the mind is stripped, searched and cuffed.

Forests burn within my sight.
Ashes fall across my shaking hand.
No vision of a path to home.
No vision of the night.

Always another morning of chores.
Always the shaman's drumming in my ears.
Always the insistent journey to the spirits -
Never ever feeling at home.

Blue dragons float across my screen:
Encounters of the imagined.
But each morning my hands fall empty:
Another morning of silent waste.

Forever, hoping to become Klee's angel.
Forever, flying ahead of the burning wastes.
Forever, in tears of longing to recover the archive.
Forever, lost to burning time.

NOURIEL'S SHOES

Nouriel does not know time wasting.
She does not know carelessness.
Asylum seekers - she cannot forgive them,
For buying their way to freedom,
For walking past crying millions in the camps.
And the lawyers, who parade
Their bookish rights, like flash cars,
She despises.

She fled Kabul in '79,
An educated woman in a liberal society
That just did not take.
Paris schooled her for a time -
Just like Khomeini, another exile -
Before the Great Southern Land
Gave her freedom,
But not a home.

She remembers Kabul:
Its ordered streets and fruit-trees,
The women laughing in the sunshine,
The children dressed in fine cottons,
Playing in the gardens.
Then, the tanks, the shells, the war, the hatred
That brought Afghanis to this kitchen,
At the other end of the world.

Here she returned the gift:
Making scarred men into kitchen hands;
Running English classes for the women;
Outwitting the men who would wrap
Their women in silent ignorance
To cocoon their cards and drink and faith;
Nouriel's freedom must be worked for.

To those many who do,
She gives all that she can.

Now she returns to Kabul,
After the Taliban
Have fled her city for now.
In abandoned parks, children play bare-footed
Between rubble and shells.
Schools barely hold their girls against poisoned faiths.
To these schools she decides to give;
So no more Afghanis will flee to her rich refuge,
But stay in her remembered home.

She buys the children shoes,
Hundreds of boxes of shoes.
One summer she visits a school with her gifts.
Watching as the children begin their long walk home,
She sees one girl carrying her box,
Still bare-footed, in the hard dust of the street.
Nouriel asks: "Why don't you put them on?"
The girl replies: "I must wash my feet first."

THE STATE OF POLITICS

Dr Cogito is reborn
Amidst our gadgets,
Displaying pixelated ruin
For ceaseless fireside chats.

On a panel two figures say:
Disunity is death is inevitable
Is the pragmatic choice
Because we know
There is no alternative.

Dr Cogito jumps to the mike
But the queued questioners
Repudiate reason
Putting passion first
To complain of taxing the elements.

Every questioner must twit the panel
To try 144 characters of fame
To display their chosen name
To win the acid-tongued mobs.

On the panel two figures say:
We hate our shrunken state
If only clear air would set us free
From all this aimless hate.

Dr Cogito taps his tablet - but too slow
The dark grieving for Lycidas begins.
Unforgiven. Blue bloody murder
Patrols these dark Scottish halls.

Dr Cogito hears *Das Rheingold*'s opening note,
And so the story goes:
We still dig from deep water's mud:
The ring, the ring, the ring.

TIMBUKTU

The old doorman put the papers in rice bags.
He carried them like old junk to the barge.
Across the river the resistance gathered
To distribute the manuscripts to private homes
Safe from the burning faith.

The Tuareg rebels - stern desert radicals
Who had forbidden dance and drum -
Slept by night in the archive,
Behind the doorman's post,
In this fortress of paper,
Drifting in drunken bloody dreams.

In the day they ploughed the mud-brick
Mausoleum into dust.
Before the captains
Began to burn the scrolls
That concealed sufi saints like chiding ghosts.
Mere paper was declared an enemy of faith.
The rich custodians in other states,
Unknown to the doorman, cursed:
"Let UNESCO shit its pants."

A longer battle resumed, in the fire,
Between sage and warrior, in Africa's heart,
Where, in 1493, the manuscripts say,
"the Tuaregs began to raid
and cause havoc on all sides.
The Malians, bewildered by their many depredations,
refused to make a stand against them"

Manuscript C was stolen decades ago.
The French took its stories of old Mali
To their looters' deposits

Where now scholars, with no tradition of their own,
Preserve this disintegrating past
In an everlasting digital sleep.
But no manuscript is innocent
Not even this doorman's sack -
When the rebels turn time into a verdict.
So, Abdurrahman As-Sadi sings:
*'I saw the ruin and collapse of the science of history.
I observed that its gold and small change
were both disappearing.'*

Yet the caretakers of old Mali
And Songai and ancient Ghana
Stopped the French stealing their past.
Simple men, orphaned children of shocking wars,
Doormen of a deeper faith,
Hid the manuscripts in desert ground,
In adobe homes,
In old bags on barges,
Until the warlords passed.

Remember the tale of the slave woman,
Buktu and her deepest well.
Ahmad Baba al-Sanhaji sings again:
*"Salt comes from the north,
gold from the south and
silver from the country of the white men;
but the word of God
and the treasures of wisdom
are only to be found in Timbuktu."*

POWER

Ritual murder is cloaked
In other names
These days.

The ghosts of the victims
Still walk in office,
Off to new exciting roles.

The high priests still brandish their knives,
Slumped sullen in the corner chair,
Spitting out their silent spite.

The screams of the fallen are suppressed
By the counters and the climbers
Who live for aimless conspiracy.

Babble mutes the grieving tear
As tea and cake
Farewell and deceive.

Each unknown fallen mandarin
Lies unmarked and dishonoured
By the prowling vermin of power.

HISTORY

We call it the judgment of history,
But no bench sits. No advocate argues,
Nor objects. No sentence is ever passed,
Except to declare the forgetting of all names.
Vainglory rests in our present flaws,
Not the archives, where stand
The buried army of the past.

Imprisoned in paper cells and steel walls,
Deprived of touch and breath,
This army weeps behind crumbling paper veils.
Their only visitor is the beguiled seeker
Who walks through the air seal's breach -
Doctor Cogito in dustless white gloves.

He searches for the scrap of spirit
That makes the song that they will sing,
And, by singing, betray its double.
The never-rooted, comic-gestured song
Haunts the burial ground;
The fleeing angel in the fiery wind
Wails and tears helplessly at her wings.

Then we, who stand on firmer ground,
Who live obsessed with the flurry of this world,
Betray the naive trust of the dead and gone.
We speak their parts all wrong.
We pull apart the broken toys of our world.
We fail, but leave traces in sacred ground.

THE CRUEL SEASON

Stranded magnolia before cream pale brick veneer
Like a naked stalk that sings its flower but once a year.

There is a time you know your time will never come
When only this short scented season saves you from

Endless text and mindless *Nō*.
We sing, we chant, but do not know.

Fallen petals, white and plum, first victims of spring,
Grace this verge, now merely a place
By which strangers walk to sing.

SEALS OF SILENCE

If ever these words should break their seals of silence,
Falling from their hidden place to be found along the
    street
Some stranger would, unbidden within the terms of
    this sheet,
Collect my fallen grace, my coded heart, into some
    secret alliance.

Then unknown knowledge would summon me again
From this dead chamber, where only memories sing,
Where I dwell within a broken house of being.
If then these words, no longer sealed, no longer silent,

But kissed with blessings, blessed with faithless spirit,
Should float to another plane,
Where the dead, stripped of costume, reign,
They will meet their lost friends, speaking of the
    infinite.

Precious dream, encircle me now, and in bitter seals
Wrap this failing speech to sing down these walls.

PRAYER

I bought a book of prayer to understand
The poetry of the spirit,
The imitation of Christ.

But prayer does not translate to my mind.
It loses me at the first trope.
It stands alone in a lightless lane.

Yet the songs of the church, its bells and choirs,
Move me without speaking,
Move me without understanding.

Untranslated,
They intimate Christ.

FORGOTTEN STORIES

We are forgotten stories, falling down,
Having drunken stronger stuff than truth.
Our past is weft, our present warped.

We feel for the braided songs that will answer
The yearning that cannot cease, flowing ever new.

Our revenants guide us where our senses fail.
We walk by the shoulder of the old Virgil,
In oblivious bliss, to a last circle of hell,
Stripped of consoling names, of the gods' own city.

Junk everywhere; abundance lies trashed
By vandals too favoured to long for the beyond.
Only apocalypse will bring us ending -
But we sing day in of loves, day out of games.

None have been older than we who stand here fallen.
None have lived more in memory's failing.
Yet still we caress the faded cloth we inherit
With numbed fingers and blinded mouths:
Following the whispered arcane secrets
Of the unbidden, unspoken, undone last song.

LAMENT

The cancer broke every part but one.
Its violence whereof we dare not speak
Frightens us into timid talk
Of happy times and dear Lycidas in drag.
For who would not cry out in pain?
Well she knew the mirror's song.

But barely knew herself the lyre's art
But tried her hand at magazine prose.
Yet, the lawyer's easy logic and fluent fraud
Never sat well with her
Notwithstanding worldly gifts.

In facing death, a deeper dark
Grew beyond the reach
Of childish friends, still talking sex.
There within, afraid and alone,
Smouldered the growing part.
There within, despite loss all around
Stood the part that purely spoke.

There within, death's best laid plans
Faltered year on year.
Cancer defied. Cancer revered,
For ten years past her death sentence.

Enough to survive.

To taste bitter juice every day
despite food becoming the disease's friend.

To see ideals broken
as her generation governed like fools

To smell the bay's salt and weed
pilling on the shore at summer's refuge

To hear her daughters speak from the scroll
and embrace the soul, as she did too, if late.

To touch a lily one last time
and bring its delicate poison to her lips.

Enough to endure one last insult
When Narcissus abandoned pain in a panic
To flee into a boyhood's dream.

But at last, alas and at once,
Despite days of terminal restlessness,
The moth swooped down
To steal her voice.

KADDISH

The wounded Narcissus does not do grief well,
Speaking tirelessly of lust at a funeral.
Prizes and awards now mock them;
The disease disappointed their glittering ambition.

The children do not mask their grief
Yet are asked to perform as the straight man
To the vanity of this generation:
"We will be there to tell you stories about your mum."
But what stories does Narcissus tell?
Coffee-shops where boyfriends tattle,
Famous names from defeated politics,
And so it goes in this low register.

The parents are silenced at this *minyah*:
No father's lament, no mother's *kaddish*,
But for the forlorn song spoken by the child
The waifs and orphans have taken over grief
To retell their illusions
To flatter themselves for not the last time.

No-one faces the darkness,
No-one stares down the disease.
The one step beyond
Into the dominion of the most high
Is beyond the ken of all but the Rabbi
Whose spoken solemn psalm alone
Tolls the bell for each departing angel.

FAITH

Reading the early history of the Christians
Fails me.
Standing alone in a Siberian church
Saved from Communism
Holding icons from 300 years ago
Fails me.
The contrition of the mighty
The passion of the fallen
The tongues of the chosen ones
All fail me.
Stoic Marcus. Zen Basho. Modern masters.
These mark a path
For Mind, not Spirit
But Bound in the Body
Cleansed of all yearning for
Magnificence.

LAST POST

Google is looking
To close your accounts after death
Like a tidy archivist sealing fragile ruins
To silence the bugle of your last post.

SELF PORTRAIT

Sweating
Cramped in a two seater
Beside a fat sleeper
I speculate on my future.

Knowing I am lost
Astray
A broken floating reed
Approaching the last years of my career

Never headhunted
Never wanted beyond small circles.
These waves of despair
Leave me alone and forgotten

A dishevelled rushed middle aged man
Whose mind cannot do things it loves.

SEAM

Below thinking
There is an oily seam.
A viscous Brisbane line,
Warm and unstable.

Contact is rare
With this substance.
We gauge its movements
With dials and sound

Translating the seeming patterns
Into certain images.
Yet those who have dug
To the bottom of thought

Who have split its seal
With reckless tools
Know the black seeping seam
Is held within no word.

THE BURNING ARCHIVE

"George Steiner, George Steiner
You called it. You called it."

I was called - was there no one better?
The flames sear my falling face.

Fragments everywhere. Things
Fall apart - like they always do.

Memory is no salve.
Not even my foreign nightingale.

In the distance a piano plays
Gymnopédies.

As if lost - I walked too far.
Collapsed. A late *auto da fé*.

I dreamt of *Uqbar,*
Dived into a mirror of fire.
Now, she speaks of Saint Petersburg
Where Raskolnikov liberated the idea,

The bloody idea that unites victim and oppressor
In this forgotten sacred space,

Where she speaks in an infinite conversation.
"Will the books escape this fire?"

The radiant heat overwhelms me.
I fall into ash, gasping for air.

An illumination of the Book of Kells
Flies by on blackened wings,

Released into the storm to die.
A whirlwind of ash climbs the heat,

Scatters all we know of time
To the wild western winds.

I crawl behind a rock and dig
Into the damp earth,

Sing the old incantations of humanity,
Paint my face with tears

And ashen flowers,
And begin my testimony.

I was born too late for fairy tales,
Too late for the theories of Freud and Marx,

Into a world that would spurn scholarship.
I sheltered in this archive -

Reader number 49 -
Where I raised my lyre among shadows.

I spoke with ghosts of the living night.
I wrote certain of my books.

I entered the order of the insane,
Under the protection of the last quisling

Who cared for the power of the sacred breath.
But he betrayed me and the angels

Who soar above our murders,
Always in tears, always looking back.

His hand signed the orders
To burn the archive down,

To clean our contemporary minds
Free of those annotated stains.

Then, she whispered to me,
For the first time:

"Live in the skies and watch the fires
Destroy your time.

Be ready for flight on the storm
blowing from paradise."

I returned to the city
As a lonely reader.

I sang on the streets for coins
To help the victims of the fires.

I searched the city of forgetting
For a new patron

Who might will
Becoming into Being.

By day I dressed as a killer
And as a penitent by night

Until the archive was closed by orders
Of the committee for public safety

To protect all good citizens
From contamination by the mind of the past.

Then all songs to the angels were outlawed
All transcendence forbidden.

I cried on the wire fence circling the fire site
Where the stories of the world were condemned.

A red-lettered notice hanged
With this warning:

"They no longer kept up
With the times."

Then, I found my courage - all that matters in the end.
I broke and entered the ruined archive

To steal the index I had written
In a black notebook

Of forgotten flowers of the mind.
With ash-stained hands, I hold it now,

Committing to the memory
That will die with me,

Like Anna's Requiem,
Spoken quietly over tea and cigarettes,

In an apartment beyond cruel history,
And its blind trust in events,

The lines of sung speech
That will endure the fire

In the arms
Of the fleeing angels.

NO FIXED POSITION

The governing world breaks apart
While from no fixed position
I reassemble affiliations between ideas.

Never knowing what is left, what is right.
At times radical, liberal and conservative
But economically always perplexed.

Call me stupid, call me confused.
History escapes the boundaries
Set by partisan adventures.

DATA

It is not Babel, but a second inundation.
Texts circling texts that shadow texts
That have long forgotten the thing itself.

Another panel springs forth with every minor idea,
Every petty writer on a speaking tour,
Where names contend in ignorance,

Where commentary smothers thought,
Where ideas tank as postures,
And in a desperate act of comprehension

Even humanists convert every notion to data.
Words abstracted to number
Twitter feeds read by API

The chatter of the crowd visualised
In scatter plots, bubbles and stars.
The speeches of a nation are counted,

Then converted to a reading score.
This binary scribble survives with no archive
As a digital trace in the clouds.

So in our I-souls
Angels have returned
The self is redeemed

Yet words have become mere data.

INVITATION

You cut open life with a paper knife
Slip out the card, a little scared
Of its embossed invitation.

But the post has been slow.
The party is almost done.
You make other plans.

MONEY FREE

Spending money used to give allure to time
But now stands across the threshold
Like a bouncer at a strip joint.

Now we find allure in our own making:
A day spent in sword and sorcery with my son,
Swimming with the accidentally discovered dolphins
At summer's suburban beach,
Inventing new rules to play monopoly
By adding cooperation and government stimuli
To the game of ruthless competition.

We turn down another forgotten restaurant meal
To swim in surf and watch birds at dawn.

AFTER SHELLEY

The unacknowledged legislators of the world
Are not the poets
But the silenced officials
Who despite the gags tied weakly to their chins

Make more of *amor mundi*
Than any idiot pontificator
Who has sucked his way
To get ass pro before his name

SUNDAY MORNING

It is Sunday morning.
No oranges go with the coffee,
No peignoir, no spirits lingering.
But I lie frightened by things to be done.

It is the morning too
When I scrape from dishes
An hour or two
To dwell in the house of being.

Dug into a warm hole
My vision finds lost thoughts,
Neglected ethics,
Abandoned dreamt life.

Chased away by chores,
Overwhelmed with failure of my days,
Gould's humming over Goldberg
Guides me again to the well.

WEEKEND FOOTY

Easter comes, and we rise again:
Our weekends infused with radio poetics,
The march to the ground,
The pies in the cold,

Standing behind the goals at the juniors,
The pipes player marching on,
The inquisition probing the deeper goals,
The champions who could have been.

This rite of rebirth,
When every season renews dimmed hope,
That this one could be the year,
Rises in the great Southern City's heart.

THE CHINESE ANCIENTS

The ancient Chinese poets
Observed their world,
As rulers do,
Detached and regretful,
Knowing action's bite.

They fled the courts
Who abused their gifts,
As rulers do,
Making words into tools,
Numbers into debts.

In exile, in refuge,
They revealed secrets,
As rulers never do,
That endure defeat
To humble the governing will.

DIFFICULTY

In my unheated room
Long difficult books
Stare from the shelves
Where they lie

Waiting for my thoughts
To cross this enchanted river
Enclosed in ice
Beyond the last post.

RE CANTO

It is not hard for me to recant
So many things I have said
So many thoughts I have forgotten

Your stare becomes an academic plea:
Time to die, you say.

You stalk me with a digital trace

I have succumbed to folly and fallacy
My arms are tattooed with illusions
My walk betrays
My habit of servile service
To greater voices, duller minds.

LONG HABITS

In time long habits will bind your feet
In sickly tape
Suckering your skin with sticky white
And leave your soul

To stand like a helpless fan
As you replay the same mistakes.
The hissy fit darkens the day
However light later words

That explain: never time, too much to do.
Burden, duty, chores and work
Ride across the sun-filled room.

THE FOREST

The child is lost in the forest.
She has taken the left path:
Lichen and lilting brooks drew her away.
She sits now disconsolate,
Her calls left alone.

The child begins to sing to the forest.
Her voice bows the trees:
Fairies carry her away to her home.
The trail of her new song
Pierces the sealed dark.

The father finds the child in the forest.
His hand embraces her fading voice:
His hold rescues her body and silences her dream.
She returns in his arms to their car.
But the song will never leave the forest.

BELATED

I am a belated one
At 47 at last a room of my own
Now I wear long shirts over
The scars of mother's tears
The words have always waited for me
Deep within my guts
Now they come, resurgent and bold
Too known to care
For publishers' judgments.

ODE TO COFFEE

Black murky mud left in a glass reveals
The source of the morning revival, as if earth
Were mined for its taste and its pharmacy

Companion to mistaken words
Witness to each morning's stumbling beginning
You wrap my hands in blue china warmth

Diseases escape your watch
Vigilance hankers for your energy
Eyes that weep with fatigue

Know that you will revive
Not only the dwindling attention
Of the over-worked

But also the in-dwelling familiar
You speak all languages
In your darkened milky croon

You bring all sorts
Before mirrors and stools
In an altar in Bourke St

Where a rich family serve
In shatter-proof glass
Your tradition made urban.

THE UNWRITTEN BOOK

Your secret will die with me, never-ending tome,
Without interrogation of your catechism.

Together we conspire for a life of dull ease,
Turning away from office, plastic and chatter,

To find in lazy days St Antony's precedent -
The world can change when we withdraw from this
      forged world.

You demand devotion and you rarely praise -
Each effort falls into silence, succumbs to depth.

Never knowing your reader, never striking home,
Never pronouncing those words you read quietly right.

Yet you stand within me, a ruin demanding speech
To interpret interpretation in spite of

The ripples of silence that cross my bedevilled
Serotonin machine. Disaster is written

In fragments, scarred by stars, in a sealed, bound text
That lies obscurely in wait for my failure.

But you will not trap me there: you will fail, not I.
The book will become a vision, broken with bread.

MONDAY MORNING

Three strikes on the snooze button
Then unwilling, still dark within,
I step out to stretch my stiff back
And you tell me - time to wake up.

This day I might return to bed;
Other days I will trudge to work.
But the self is the task today:
Verse, rest, reflection, dreaming on

These shards that dwell within my mind.
The unbuilt felt magnificence,
Looming over the central square,
Announces the will to be built.

SKIVING OFF

Skiving off is what you do
When leaving work at four
The boss throws a glance

Through the glass and on you go.
It does you good
Now and then.

THE BURNING ARCHIVE - THE END

Destruction
       Ruins of ruins of ruins
              Abandoned broken words

The commentators will say there is no other way.
The fact of the matter is we know we do not know.
We know we will fall.

The flames leap higher and higher.
A Japanese town melts away,
Its officials hide in deceiving words.

Drumming. Screaming.
Wires screeching across the sky.

All meaning is shattered now.
All voices break here.

The frames are falling in flame.

A small angel flies with blue wings,
Singing a lullaby in front
Of the roaring dust and ash.
Her light hair is knotted.
She sings a frail note in the whirling wind.
The flames will always haunt her.

Time is torn in two.
Broken. Lost. Deserted.
The path has been lost.
Words fall to sleep.

He sat with his face buried
In his twisted fingers, and

Cried for the words -
And the sense that he had lost.

In his tower he sat and
Gathered the words he had written
Over the decades.
He had notebooks and scraps
And cards and files and paper.
Nothing at all was whole.
Nothing was finished.
It did not find his ambition.
He felt sickened by all the scrawl.

Write less; find silence:
He spoke in tears.

He saw himself cut his own throat
With a cook's knife. Then
Fall into a bath of blood.

What hope, what purpose, what steady rope
To hold onto each morning?
What does become of the broken-hearted?

Error, not class
Is the engine of history

What voice survives the burning archive?

This world was lost.

PART FOUR

DR COGITO'S REBELLION
2016-2018

LIFE EXPECTANCY

At fifty-one I sleep in loss
Broken at last on fortune's wheel
To ninety-one I wander with a pauper's plan
No early grave to relieve my failing heart
My cerebellum longing for more serotonin
My fingers still restlessly searching
Through these ghostly keys

Do I expect in forty years
To see the world turn and break again
The purity seal
My eleven year old child
Wrapped around my fate?

Will great words return again
Salvaged from our wretched wreck
By toiling troubadours?

Will walls fall? Will heroes sing?
Will we see Mao's kind again?
Will money lose its hard-won shine?

Or will these years slide on by
As I recede into comfort?
Will oblivion be my friend at last?
Will silence guard my end?

All I know is one more day.

DR COGITO'S REBELLION

Dr Cogito wailed to the wall:
Banished I am. Banished from the sun.
Yet in exile is freedom, where beauty is won.
Rise, strange city, with me, in revolt.

But the wall did not fall.
The prowling police only smiled askance,
As they waved on the disturbance;
Just one stranger cried, for no real reason at all.

So, Dr Cogito roamed the city by day,
A lone man, with misshapen hair,
His beard dull white, his track pants stained with piss.
He dictated wild revolt to his handheld device.

His mind let go of all hierarchy,
Swooned upwards into the swirl of dream,
And from the ashen scarred sky
He dictated the fleeing angel's decrees.

Flail the pleasure-seekers. Let blood mingle with
    come.
Hang the merchants by the weight of their debts.
Empty the archives, and make a wild pyre
There to burn the courtiers whose brand I wear here.

To his arm he then pointed:
A blackened and bruised star,
The mark of the accursed,
The outcast's pride jewel, he cried.

Then in waiting for savagery again to roam the earth
At last, in fear, the crowd attended
To this homeless man's address.

But no words came a-preaching, as he fell to his knees,

Only tears and crumbling muscle,
As he looked afar, to the angel blown away by the fire.
Farewell, he sobbed, in this city we never will belong -
Before a patient nurse came to hurry him along.

DR COGITO'S NEW JOB

To the spare cubicle allotted, Dr Cogito retired,
No longer trusted, no longer on the rise.
He had confused his station, mistook himself for best.
Now stripped of all power,
He should have known better.
He should have let it rest.
No bells from the Ethernet, no projects from on high
Just a long wait till termination,
Till forgetting, till dusk,
Spent respelling illusions,
Wasted serving dull cant,
Making humdrum gangsters seem spry and fresh
When they visit aged care centres
To bore solid citizens with stump speeches from hell.

Yet still on his table the world plays its acts
And in briefs he seizes his moment -
Since the lowly are best to advise the prince,
As even the great Machiavelli knew in his disgrace.

To cancel so public words is his strange fate -
To attend instead to soft voices in his head
That force him to pull over on the road,
To dictate to a memory device.
There too springs this old odd dream
That these heard voices might outlive him,
Might find their way to an ancient stone church,
And there outlive the fires.

DR COGITO ADMITS HE IS MAD

Dr Cogito admitted at last he was mad
Not anxious not depressed but quite simply mad
Abandoned by all gods
Thrown out defenceless on Lear's wide range

He had never felt so free
Never so unchained by duty and reason
No longer did his words serve
Broken men and their dog ideas

He stripped himself and stood
Alone and ashamed but no more afraid
To preach to the pigeons and the gulls
Who had fled from the frozen city's blue square

THE GLASS HALF FULL

I took a glass and placed it there
Lone and harsh in the optimistic air;

And they cried out, do not cry,
Cassandra, it is a half full glass you spy.

I wince and squint but do not see
Any liquid but glass before me.

So I declare, the glass half full right there
Is only filled with dry hot air.

Its sides are cracked.
Its lip is chipped.

Its base unwashed
Attracts insects to feed.

But my truth was scorned,
So, to the poor shadows I returned.

THE EXILE OF DR COGITO

Dr Cogito allowed himself to dream
Of the end of his long exile.
The great ones at the gate,
At last, welcomed him to the city.
He was summoned alone to the pink heath room.
Where he like Pirate Jenny reviewed the captives;
Administered death and mercy;
And spoke aloud, at last,
The judgments of the poisoned prophet.

But the dream was a lie,
Told by the same great ones
Who had toyed with Dr Cogito's unworldly visions,
His ponderous words, cast into forgotten forms.
He woke from the dream in a cell;
Bare rations, fed by the camp jailor.

Stripped of all office, all company,
A scribe in chains, with no pen, no book,
Condemned to solitary for his solitude.

For Dr Cogito, and all the dreamers,
Who burn in their precious books,
Exile never ends.

DR COGITO'S MISSION

In all the furious sounds of this last fortress
Underneath the moulded stone a darker smell begins
No song lays itself down for Dr Cogito

He must stir himself and bestride
The fields of strife
Where in some enemy's demise he loots his prize

He must abandon the regulated life
The safety of this strange city's walls
To roam in pursuit of his quarry

And when he finds a bird that strikes
Perfection in its melody
He must turn away to twisted forms

Broken words and small disguises
The *secretum secretorum*
That alone and in silence he writes

And when the mercenary princes of the besieged cities
Send for him in dreams
He will laugh in Nietzschean scorn - from his book.

PUBLIC WORDS

We blind ourselves in a swaddle of banal mouths
Our public men and women
Amidst their giggles and stunts
Stammer their faith in having no words to speak
Relentlessly talking crap

Our troubadours forsake their art
For coin and glamour

Even trauma and sacrifice in war
Defeat the voices of these mimes
No tragedies no suffering they go through
No pain beyond the reach of medicine
Can be imagined

As if public words and imagination
Were foreign lands
As if empathy was not the cardinal ordinary virtue
The chain for every now
The foundation of the republic

Fugitive and broken are these public words
Lost, but haunting, my despised gods
Destitute, these affluent times

INSOMNIA

It happens
About one or two
The worst side of midnight
Sometimes my dick. Sometimes my gut.
Bloated and sore
The snoring never helps
The knowledge tomorrow will not change
Caffeine chasers to kill afternoons
Trapped among the hollows
And the thought I will never belong

DR COGITO'S FALL

To this no-man fathomed deep,
In Dante's written hell,
Down long, down cold, to flames I fell.

To the great men in union dues
I begged revenge to ill effect,
In the plumbers room,
Where power left me sole and wrecked,
A forgotten drunk with no spine,
Nor mind, fettered to this too real city,

But reaching for the things no numbers surpass.
My words watched from outside tearful glass
The bejeweled feast I am banished from,
Where, in branded rags to hide,
I steal sobs in sunken strife.

When only the mind is wrong,
The body soon sings pain in sympathy.
Then all day is dim,
Then all day is dull -
Slowly awaiting the numb relief

Of small capsules of hemlock
That for my errors in life
I am condemned to drink
And whose illusion breaks in groggy morn.

We call the land of the drones sane.
Escorted from the hive,
Freed from the dream of a cell to call mine own,
I am left to die, labeled and useless,
Clutching only my doctor's script.

There, cowering alone I sing
Incantations of prose
To revive five forlorn bells,
An elegy to march towards weak light,
In this dread pageant stripped of mystery.

There, like an exiled, imprisoned king
I relive commiserated glories.
I pen laments and memories
Of an ill-tempered sovereign
At war with circumstance
Who lets the mad and insignificant
Moulder into a green and grey corruption
Where his true reign begins.

In the waiting room my eyes close.
I drape alone this penance,
And hide in frailty,
A long travelled pilgrim,
To wait upon the doctor's administration.
Sitting with hands cupped upwards
Eyes closed, and bleeding,
I catch by sound alone
A rain of fallen martyrs
Whose lives are not told
In magazines, big or small,
Who scream tortured in household duty.

This long life lacks rites of recurring spring.
And so we must find them in learning, in memory.
So, each successive soul can dance itself to death
To appease our productive monster.
So, in the sacrifice, the tribe is revived.
So, through sacrifice, the murmured lines endure.
What prince can promise such dire eternity?
No dreamt dwelling, this long wished home.

ONE THOUSAND STEPS

Moss covered log
Lichen robed manna moist
You fell here too
At some unstressed time
About half way up to one tree hill
Beyond the battles inscribed in this journey
Near the pass and the crossing, nameless now,
The end still one thousand breaths away

Still but never in silence
The log allowed the moss to grow
To make evergreen ears in the thousands
And here to attend to the forest fall
Near vertical lines screen all
But glimpses of the strangers' city
In this percussive forest of symbols

And to my eyes so is all I see
Notwithstanding the city ken
Cockatoos white and black
Scream their way to Walhalla
An engine whines its solitary death
And the lyre parodies the rancour
Of sports militias training up and down
In their industrial silks
Barely forgiving the mindful walkers

But alone on this wryly named hill
With its scraped bald pate
Two workmen lunch in silent hi-vis vests
And two walkers stop for rest
And learn to listen

NO MARKERS

There are no markers for when I pass
To this world that holds me fast

But permits at least with frequent trips
Brief reports on conditions there

Most of the lands are unmapped
The cities blur in broken memories

The smouldering glory of a world undone
But for ruins curated by my kind

It is the simple things I can repeat
Like slicing slowly through a peach

Or standing atrophied
In complete exhaustion

Before the verdicts of my peers collapse
And hard men learned in the ken

Cry out for me to run, and take
These poor letters to unknown friends

Breathing hard and fast I wait upon
Their answer heard alone in the other world

At other times they call me outcast
In ashen dress I conceal my crime

Perhaps even I have forgotten
What marked me what called me

To sit in feigned solitude
And demand a prophet's vision beyond my strength

Yet these self-sworn chains
And the blistered skin beneath

Are now my nightly gown my stately dress
No laughter no canon of the humane

No death can free me from this daily task
To transmogrify the unattainable madness

Then in Hakluyt editions of some second life
These strange journeys will encounter

The welcoming arms of the prodigal father
At last taste unquenchable life with dear Penelope

LEUCOXOLYN

White wood makes
An offering in an urn
Pink fringed ghost caps

BARREN BOOKS

We who in barren books
Seek the things beyond green ken
There we see the dead learned stele

Gold clasped naiad
Enslaved in display
Social Medea.

UNRIBBONED

Staunchly unribboned
Unbadged unpinned
I march lonely
Down a shadowed street

No banner
No masthead
No digit
No mark
Only intimated voices
That visit in these moments

When the crowd within
Clears away
And then
I stand only here alone

UNREALISTIC ATTEMPT

The controlling umpire ran towards the fallen man
Blowing his whistle, calling out his shame:
Unrealistic attempt.

The fallen man had jumped far too soon
And stumbled over air and backs
Like a clown mime in a busker gig.

The ball had floated high above
Well beyond his reach
And his brief flight

Ended before any chance
To grasp in a single pluck
The red god from the suspended air.

So the fallen man
Crumpled in his athletic gaffe
Derided by opponents and crowd alike

Now earns a failure's stripe
The condemnation as the men in white
Cry out: unrealistic attempt.

But how do the men in white
know the ambit of the jumper's dream
in the moment before the launch?

How can they know the accidents that may come
from knees and backs and upward thrust,
And so might make the desperate leap last

So that grace and fortune, this one time,
Would hold the fallen man a few seconds more
In hang time's eternal zone?

They cannot know
But can only judge
With fierce sanctity
The treason
Of the unrealistic attempt.

BLACK SALT SEA

When death yearns and reaches its graven hands
For my exhausted heart, and I twist life
Into clay models, icons of madness,
Servants of my neural demiurges,

Then I stand alone on this eroded shore
Where I sing threnodies to the conquering waves.
My songs sink beneath the foam and froth
That dances across the black salt sea.

There they drop down to a new sunken life
Preserved in brine, hidden from sun and wind,
Drowned eternally in secret shame,
Solemn silence beneath ever darker tides.

HOOP OF RESCUE

I was only nine when they shamed me.
The girl led me on and they all were in.
What seemed love and beauty was just a trap.
Pillory and laughter. Mockery and scoff

Blackened by primary schooled heart.
A ring of abuse was chill-marked
On my grained wood. Friendly society
Cut me loose, and I drifted alone

In a bark down the tear-treacle course,
No hoop of rescue ever to hold.

THE MORNING NEWS

The talk today is of war and civil strife
Jacked cars and hijacked souls
Shootings, beheadings and preachers of hate
Two parties shouting across a beige panel

A drowned child sacrificed to fear and spite
Fissured identities spelled out in letters
Too long and too changing to hold fast the past.
Bombs that tear open concrete hearts

Of ancient cities we no longer know
Two men in windcheaters rape a babe
A grieving maddened child submits to death
In a SUV that is filmed on its way
To a scarred and deserted paradise.

WHEN THE WIND BLOWS FROM I KNOW NOT WHERE

When the wind blows from I know not where
And stained visions crowd my troubled sleep
I wake late, mistaken and stripped bare
Only to stumble on the rock where I am told to leap

Leap into words infinite and sentences dread
Into equations of the unreal and forbidden
Into these whispers that press past me like strangers
In a city, where even the streets are made of ether,

And where I land and if and why
Are not mine to know

I land in some foreign place
Unimagined and unplanned
An accidental tourist
Chained in chance again.

SNOW FALLS ON THE SUBURBAN PLAIN

Snow falls on the suburban plain.
I shelter, wrapped in a library of wool.
The prophecies of last winter
Stand unproven before me.

Was the doom of governments so sure?
Did the blood-dimm'd tide swell and fall
On the innocence of the world?
Who, if anyone, escaped the burning of books?

Ashamed of error, I dismiss my men
To walk stooped and love-shorn
To the silent shore of the undreamt world
Where I cast my runes again.

Who is Zarathustra with no omens?
Who will heed my hammered song?
As snow turns sleet turns rain,
The runes speak only of pain.

THE YEARS DRAG ON BEYOND MEASURE AND FORM

The years drag on beyond measure and form
The story long ago anticipated its own end
Every question posed, is just that
Even the chorus silently winks to applause

Reality itself no longer suits so well
Despite our sour pretence and cynic's sad grin
We augment the insufficient world
With the ghosts of our trickster gods

Every place is laden with too much known
Every known is unknown by the all too knowing
Our eyes cede sight to cameras in phones
Our minds forsake sweet memory for google

But our tongues still claim the power of speech
Whose rites and ceremonies stir a deeper world
Of unreason and music and madness afire,
Still performed in cruel circles, hidden at night.

THE WORLD RESEMBLES AN ETON MESS

The world resembles an Eton mess
Its sweetened peaks
Used for second-hand meals
Crushed and adrift
On Chantilly cream
Strawberries and jam
In random casts
Complete
This shattered poetry

THE TETHERED MIND

The mind prowls, tethered to its past.
An unknown unknown rises alone
From unclaimed graves of fidgetty glances.
The waves come for the fallen swimmer

Again and again. They roll fast.
They suck his feet into the undertow.
A macadamia tree in a shadowed grove,
Where dreams were made,

Rots and blackens, drowned below
The lapping murk of Brisbane's spill.
Something else happened there.
Something I cannot sit with.

Cannot say, not even now, not at all,
But for the leather, chafing my neck in thrall.

DR COGITO AT WORK

March on into the marshes
For you have no choice.
Choices are for slaves.
Your duty is to sit with the dying

And obey. Always obey.
Obey the blonde aides-de-camp
Whose orders echo in your mind
Like trite i-pop songs.

Leave the traitors behind.
Sing your own lay,
To honour the fallen, the broken,
The destitute, the mad, your own
Compatriots in miserable truth.

You will never belong.
Cut yourself free from the idea
That a general will stop you on the march
To pin some stripes to your caved in chest.

But keep marching.
March till your legs collapse beneath you.
Then rest in whatever mud or dust
Offers you a home.

And sleep that night
As if it were your last.
Dream and watch lucidly
While the poison drains into the soil.

LONG SUMMER

Another long summer
Dead leaves litter the paths
Of the lost wanderers

EXECUTIVE

She flicks through lines
On a stylish device
No eye contact
In the restless lift
Then speeds
With blinkers on
Her ideas to some
Ineluctable finding.

DR COGITO BROUGHT HIS MIND TO HEEL

Dr Cogito brought his mind to heel
And made a long, dark inventory list
Of all the errors of his errant mind.

The unfinished manuscript on dark power.
The poems that returned formality
To its accustomed esteem.

His escape attempts,
Breaking from his lifelong cell,
To reach into the charmed circle

Where the potentates dwell.
Broken diets. Failed regimes
That exercised his core strength.

Abandoned readings. Forlorn petitions
To those who do belong
In some salon or cafe in the great city

Where the infinite conversation
Proceeds in exalted time,
Somewhere beneath his daily dream.

The one time he interpreted Borges
As a fantasist of parthenogenesis.
The tears he spilled

On Boyd's oils at Shoalhaven.
The winters - so many -
When the dim tide of his missing salts

Lapped the memory of a drowning child.
His ravings to the ethernet
On the latest thing he had read.

All the distractions from true purpose.
The fears that penned him.
His cravings for sweets.

The mentors he might have had,
If he were not like Parsifal
Lost and wandering through this crystal forest

In search of his once true name.
The longing for scholarship,
Its erudite footnotes and elegant forms

So out of place in this hyper-linked world.
Songs of sorrow in memory of the dead
Whose suffering he sought to know.

ROCKET MAN

I think it's gonna be a long long time

Love of child
Is unconditional
The US security man says

But that is not true
Between nations

It's lonely out in space

The winds of spring
Stir pollen into my eyes

I stop along the way
I pinch the fat
Gathered like guilt

From a bad winter of habits

I think it's gonna be a long long time

This science I don't understand
All I know is
I'm not the man
they think I am at home

On such a timeless flight.

THE POET IN A TIME OF TERROR

No words can describe this
The bodies flew up like dolls
A father spoke by phone to his thirteen year old son
When the car struck him
The politician played Augustine
He declared this an act of pure evil
But Anna's Requiem found the words
Long songs of sadness
Black-eyed Pierrots
With cigarettes clasped by lips
The old songs are lost in the sirens
And empty books broke memory
In this world a man himself is nothing
And there ain't no other world
The poet bows his head to the porcelain wall
And lets out his tears in rain
The radio repeats the same information, over and over
Until silence itself is known
As the greatest terror
The silence of early morning
Woken in fear, wretched and worried
The closer you are to Caesar the greater the fear
Every city is stained
Code names substitute pen names
No skalds now. No epics.
The old songs are forgotten.
The poet sits in the gutter.
Trembles. Mutters bits and pieces.
Who can write poetry after this?
Who cannot?
The real heroes stand by the wounded.
Heal them.
Speak kind words
In their agony.

Drive the ambulances
To the hospital beds.
One off-duty policeman
Pulled open the door
Of the vehicle of attack
Prised out
The jihadist madman, the addict
- Or was he just an impulse
A storm of grievance
Inside a prison mind -
Wrestled him into arrest.
What point do threnodies serve?
I am not even Marlow
On the Thames,
Accepted in my strangeness.

DR COGITO REGRETS THE FUTILITY OF HIS EXISTENCE

Do not believe your search will end
Only in salted bread
And a place as a stoker somewhere

The commanding heights will never know
The impress of your shoddy boots
You will die in this open plan

There will be no obituary for you
In our forgotten press
No flowers cast from famous hands

Only the well-known taste of clay
The executioners will gossip
At your grave your madness

Your uncomfortable squirming
When asked to lie
To play along with the latest

Comrade from the rainbow guard
Your dated learning
All those useless books

What help were they
When the judges took your eyes
As if the law could take your side

Only silence forgetting betrayal
You wandered blind prophet
Searching the way
To the castle and back

You never knew
All lies
Every last veil
Do not believe your helpless revenge

Will disturb the board as it meets
Your words became chains
Holding you against invented change

It was that they distrusted
Words that flowed too well
Bonds between mind and burning soul

Evidence of your jihad
The print on your weapon
Their last conspiracy

Will be to end your words
To make memory fail
To disperse the last rain cloud

And they will say
Do not believe.

DR COGITO STRUGGLES AGAINST HIMSELF

No sooner than one word lands on the page
Than fear of revenge strangles any song
Dr Cogito sits silently in fear
He thinks writing is still dangerous
The way he practises it
The hollow men will come
To make him pay
None will thank him for his bitter letters.

PEACHES IN A BOWL

There it stands
The Indian metal bowl
Silver outside
Burnt orange and black streaks

Glossed in its basin
Inside arranged with care
Each sticker taken from the skin
Eight peaches and five nectarines

It stands
In the middle
Of the long table
Where we talked

Where we laughed
Where we played
Where we cried
Where we became who

It stands alone
In the late afternoon light
The only thing
You need to know on this earth

Filling the air with scent
Before your flight
It stands there
Until your return.

ELEGY

There is no world but this one,
Yet we are incomplete;
Left stranded and voiceless

When the anima disappears in the sea.
Helplessly, we cry out to memory
Since there is no other belief:

Farewell. Thank you. And hear this pledge:
We will remember you.
But the broken sessions of truth-telling

Are lost forever now, though I may coddle
Silent fantasies for years.
The words between us land in weak memory.

No consecration by presence.
No darting eye of thought.
No castigation by madness.

Merely fading recollections.
Merely words, written down.
Merely sweet sanctioned sentiment.

No more Sunday phone calls.
No more complaints about your health.
No more fears of tipping into hypomania.

After the flood, the illness
Possessed your inutile mind.
Decades followed in sterile locked wards.

Exiled from the Glasshouse Mountains,
Stranded, far from home,

You suffered the worst of tragedies,

And died too much alone.
Few attended your funeral, but there they saw
A young woman who before they never knew:

Photos of Dido before her betrayal.
And so the floating bier was lit
By a soaring arrow of words aflame.

And your ashes will mingle with the ocean,
While we stumble towards the same fate,
Muttering insane love for the world bereft.

A HISTORY OF MADNESS

Dr Cogito read Foucault like a madman
In search for the silent stones,
Hidden in the lake

Where sails the Narrenschiff.
He peoples his history with memories:
His cold companions from dread literature,

The rare voice of the mad known to history,
His ill-chosen friends who have succumbed.
To them all he says, we are split, split are we.

When did it begin, Dr Cogito asks?
Did it even ever?
Was it some event in childhood, the brain, the genes?

She fell from a tree. The blow to the head,
Could that explain neurology's enigmas?
Or is it banishment from our kind that says it all:

The outcast's laments
The leper's cross
The madman's curse.

Dr Cogito made heroes
Of the rebels
Against reason;

Chanted their words
Painted their screams
Endured their agonies.

He uttered to be done with the judgment of God,
As if that would distinguish him.

But what help were the images of Foucault?

When you spoke with her
In the locked ward
Of the psychopolis at Larundel?

There, Dr Cogito learned Foucault
Was a barren sadist; his ideas, mere whips
To lash the world for his own joy.

Dr Cogito wondered - can you make madness identity?
To perform like a freak in a poetry slam,
To play to the hipsters' sneers and cackles?

Comfort for the squatters of the inner city,
But not the true history of his mad gang.
The authentic songs of the night journeys

Do not condemn
The helpers and carers
The witnesses of madness:

Who listen all night
to her scientific ravings;
Who endure accusations of a genetic flaw;

Who call the crisis assessment team at Christmas;
Who know their frailty astride the mind's mountains;
Who know only that the medication works.

Dr Cogito took his mind to the dark boundary
And there lost it in an absent-minded fit.
"Madness is the absence of the oeuvre",

The professor muttered
On the long journey

Back to shelter,

Where at last he would enjoy
Simple home cooked meals,
Creep under cold comfort in the wind.

To converse again in infinite lines.
To consecrate his life as an outcast.
To commit his memories to the flame.

And know the terror of the limit
That has not left madness behind
Blessed that the worst has not yet come.

DR COGITO ENTERS THE FERAL CITY

O feral city, fortress without iron gates,
Beckoner of corruption, seed of all illness,
Asylum of blessed and astonishing madness,
Take me before your therapeutic magistrates

So I may defy the law
Within the wen.
Then break my weakened chains
Flee the disordered court,

And make my way
Through alleys to the port
Where I can trade my identity
For freedom again.

Let me hear the murmur of anonymity,
That tragic chorus chanted from your broken walls.
Brace me with a black woollen coat against mistrals
That chill all your mistaken streets, cruel city.

Here, I am lost in a crowd
Of five million who like me
Only hear silent
Sneers from History.

We lose our ways on congested roads.
We do tricks for the local gangsters
Who rule but no longer pretend
To honour the reverent Law.

Crime and power, drugs and violence
Keep the streets in something they call work

Where even defrocked elites
Make a show like good little bourgeois.
What is my voice - this withered reed in a swamp -
To these criminal gangs who ransack our tradition?
It is nothing.
I know that.

Yet my weak rebellion
Against the ruin of our estate gives me the strength
To find my place in the shadows of the feral city
And send sad songs into the evergreen infinity.

PART FIVE

MEDITATIONS 2018 TO 2020

LIGHTNESS

My struggle has ended.
I sit in harmony with myself.

The rain is falling
Into the light.

Out of ruins, eternal ruins,
There walks a wanderer.

He carries a spear from another time,
Lays it across

The stone atop the waterfall
Then dives to his freedom.

HEAVINESS

This morning every muscle aches.
My quads creak like plaster casts.
My head fills with inward tears,
Unwilling to burst their dams.

Everything is too much.
The call from my sister
About the money in the will.
Clearing out junk emails.

Succumbing to the phishing.
And this dawn invites only sleep -
Even running drives me back to bed.
I am split, wrecked, lost in a tempest.

My sodden clothes pull me down.
It is ending, as it began, in the water.

LOSING MY DIRECTION

The mornings drift away now.
Spikes in my hair no more.
Seventeen seconds reminds me
The young are never right about life.

It does not matter how hard I work now
Not what I say in those moments on stage:
I am condemned now. I walk the borderline,
And my words fall into the ice.

Habit has become an iron cage now,
Where reason stalks my failures,
Where I spend my days in madness,
And Ezra chants our company into ruin.

Every night floods the purposes of the day now.
Error is all in the not done.
Now, the mornings are a swamp of the not done,
And my legs succumb to the sickening mud.

ODE TO ANOTHER NIGHTINGALE

After fifty years words still defeat me
At every beginning.
The thing itself slips from my fingers.
I am left with only solipsist phrases.

Outside the city crumbles:
All too human millions wear out the circuitry.
They pile on mountains of waste.
They discard the amanuenses of their lives

And forget the nightingale,
Whose darkling requiem pulls no crowd,
Though in this shaded room
Its song is still praised by a solitary priest.

Here alone again on this Sunday morning
Its machine-made song still
Transports the chanter from weary chores
To some secret memory of the true rites.

Forgotten and broken rites,
Interrupted by leopards,
Are rehearsed to this song
In this dark place, sheltered from the ruins.

Forlorn, he read, and strikes the bell.
But no townsfolk assemble at the church.
Only loud cackles from another room,
And this question: do we still dream?

BOUNDLESS

Is what the meditating mind
Gets to in the end,
When asked, Who am I?

And when I ask myself?
A tired lanky man in his 50s
Who has just learnt to sleep.

Player of games.
Healer.
Night Elf Priest.

Singer of dirges.
Essayist on time
And cruel forgetting.

Reader
A man lost in words
Like my relative

Whose index cards
Of the language
Kept in an outhouse

Gave the world
A perfect reference
Of order.

A failed bureaucrat
That much I know.
A man ill suited

For his times.
Neglected Cassandra
Watching his city burn.

A truly educated man
Adrift in the doldrums.
No port beckons.

No wind gathers.
There will be
No homecoming.

The ocean never ends.
We are not equal to its currents.
Its storms overwhelm us.

We can only hope
We survive the shipwreck:
To make our home on a patch of strange land.

FALLING INTO MEANING

You prepare for this moment,
Ready the attention to shift
From the tickertape of Being
To the House of Possibility.

Intentions do not rule here.
Each day begins anew with nought.
A blank screen quivering in silence
Calls me to step onto the board

Then plunge into meaning beyond
My control. I will fall
Into the obscure waters
And hope my swim makes them clear.

But it is the fall that counts most.
It is the fall that releases the past.

COUNT YOUR BREATHS

Count your breaths.
Let the strophe and antistrophe
Lull you into a calm that poses no threat.

Make of this moment a pregnancy
Full enough to know
Dharma, contentment and rest.

Breathe more slowly now
As if oxygen made the heart
Forget all the breaking pains.

Allow the mind to drift
To fallow dreams, and there
Throw the seed that redeems

This life of nightmare and shuddering fear.
Feel your body separate from your mind.
Watch as your dismembered soul

Takes to the air.
Let it drift away as your feet
Grow roots into the land.

Now bloom like Yggdrassil
From this black soil, and let it
Perch in the branches of the undying tree.

ABANDONED

The winter is howling outside this room.
The rumble of the heating returns me
To my mind, where I observe old fears loom.
Why? The anima has abandoned me.

Dreams in dust, neglected half-done paintings,
Notebooks that circle like spectres around
The trauma, familiar and forgotten,
Who marks out in song my living ground.

Three good years: when I bore dragons in fire;
When I transformed by talk my reflection;
When I crossed the desert, and did not expire,
But found my way to the infinite conversation.

They are over now, broken by an accident.
I must walk out of the underworld alone.
It was always to be that way: bent,
Broken, but reborn by a hand now gone.

Outside now, sirens are calling the world
To another emergency of fire, storm or flood.
Yet I walk in chanted silence, not alone,
But surrounded by the flowers of Persephone.

EVERY TWIST

Every twist and out of sync move
Punishes me with pangs of pain.
Had you been taught to sit? he asked
Had you learned to walk?

Suddenly crippled, my body
Still longed for motion and ease;
But each step forward overreaches.
Every leg swing causes winces.

Now just to sit before these words
And quieten the reckless mind
Invites another long struggle
With my newly stranger body.

So I too must hang from this tree
Nine nights for Odin's gift to me.

EMPTINESS

This morning when I look inside: nothing.
When I search for a string of words;
When I seek some fragment of meaning
To share in the ether world: nothing.

My projects are discarded on the street.
No scavengers pick through the rubbish
To salvage pure sentences from waste.
No-one searches for my lost precious.

All I want is to hide and to sleep.
To relinquish the pain in my legs;
For the inflammations to wash away;
To hear the sirens call my name.

THE MONSTROSITY OF POWER

Eyes make an abyss, and we swim in pain.
The iron staff, tipped in blood,
Discarded on Persian carpets,
Extinguishes the last truth of this dynasty.

The scrawled notes instructing murder
In the margins of decrees,
Urging the necessity of firing squads,
Tell the secret truth of this revolution.

The shaking voice and remembered tears
In the Prime Minister's courtyard,
After the factions take down their man,
Speak the silenced truth of this parliament.

Blue bloody murder still stalks our halls.
Into the whirlpool the dying demos falls.

NO WORDS ARE COMING TO ME

No words are coming to me today.
My legs ache, and a hazy pain
Surrounds my mind. Silence is king.
The essays of yesterday are forgotten.

Only this flawed mirror can save me:
If I can stand before it calmly,
For the duration of four stanzas,
And note down the mistakes of my soul.

There will be no hero's journey today.
Only these singing waves,
Breaking over my limp body
Pinioned in the restless sand.

Under the water I hear ancient sirens
Who I follow into the sunken tomb.

HISTORY

Nothing these days is as it seems,
And ideas… well, don't trust them.
I pore over the all too human follies
Of dynasties and revolutions,

And create like Casaubon a sterile wisdom.
Into grey garners, I pour the husks of time.
The vital seed has long since passed away.
Lost in trash, I know the madness of the day.

My towers of discarded folly stand alone
On the outskirts of the rampaging town.
Before long, the prophecies say, the dark rider
Will take me to my trial and put all I know to fire.

Then who will be left to pick through the ash?
What druid will plant the last fired seed?

SACRED SPEECH

In the grey stone chamber
The chanters sing
Threnodies that tell

Of the blood tide swell.
On mountain tops shaman
Intone stone-scrawled words.

SILENCE

I look into the black lake
And hear only silence.

I untangle the spider's web
And hear only silence.

I stare at old garners of grain,
The stores of our memory,

The wellsprings of our lives,
But hear only silence.

Is this the beginning of the end?
Do I recycle the scraps of my youth,

Spin the wheel of eternal recurrence,
Pull down old favourites from the shelf

Forever now until the moment of my death?
And what for? To end this shame?

To fill the emptiness with more meagre words?
If only these chanted lines would build a wall

To surround this scented garden
Where I sit and watch my mind decay.

Then in guarded silence, with the world in retreat,
My body rots down into the soil of the tree.

ANOTHER GENERATION

Another generation passes me by
I sit and know my time will not come.
I retreat into this room of texts
Where I imagine parleys with the dead.

Machiavelli tells me of civil strife
And the virtue that our republics forget.
He comforts me with the exile's lament:
I will not enter that walled city of which I sing.

An old and broken Max Weber,
In a bitter iron cage, speaks of authority -
Forgotten salve our elites do not possess
And only true office can restore.

And dear sweet Arnold, whose melancholy storms
Beat against these faraway beaches,
Sings of loss, beauty and unspeakable truths
That our hurried time has no time for.

I leave the infinite conversation for the day
Armed against the hungry generations
Who surround the besieged city in which I dwell
In my crumbling but invincible tower.

LATE SPRING

Last night the storming rain woke me.
The last hot day of spring ended so
In broken and forgotten dreams.

Besieged by pollen, veins awash with poison,
I sneeze and wheeze though this late spring
With memories of the Pazzi Plot

And the Opium War beside my bed.
I imagine conspiracies against New Corruption
To bring down the enemies of tradition

But let them fall to the sane ground
Like discarded tissues. Where now,
Parzival of the South? Who speaks

For the world in which you are lost?
The Golden Wattle and Waratah
Have bloomed their last late song.

There is no community for your song.
You wander alone and beyond the pale
With your Great Work wrapped in wool

And hidden behind your searing eyes.
To the barren summer you march
Like the forgotten camels of the desert.

FRIENDSHIP

The surging white waters
Carried us along for a time,
Down the snow-filled stream
Through the charred timbers

Out onto the plain of red-roofed houses
In which we spied our enemies
Talking over tea of conspiracies
And how sovereignty would use us.

The rafts began to separate
While we drifted through the last city
Spilling into the spitting sea
Whose rips and froth rent us apart.

Now sun-bleached, adrift, alone and starving
I wonder if our friendship was ever a thing?

TWITTER POEM

Language is
Breaking down
One #flaw
At a time.

Culture was
A memory,
Once, if only
To a few

Who cared.
In darkness
Now they
Burn.

In the ash
Find the flame.

BEING NOTHING

What do you write when nothing is to be done?
Who are you when you are nothing?
What is memory for when nothing endures?
Why do we go on when nothing waits for us?

Will these words be stored, with all other sweet
    nothings?
When there is nothing about them that matters?
What comes before the nothing
That smothers every hope like nothing else?

When there is nothing to affirm
Why do words still demand nothing
But to be spoken, if only about fear of nothing?
Why do we fear nothing

As if nothing else could harm us
As much as the burning city that is nothing?

THE BREATH OF LIFE

In one moment
The breath disappears

It becomes
Just that

No hanging on
No dreaming on

Pure disappearance:
Death in life

Or is it
Life in death?

THE MIND

I climb the mountain
Where only the madness lives
And take one last bloom.

I descend the barren hill
And throw petals in the wind.

RAIN FALLS IN FEBRUARY

Rain falls in February:
The burnt out town sings
In its brick circle.

WINTER PHRASES

The pill foil is done.
I have lost my haiku book
And my therapist.

Sweet sessions of memories
Cascade over the green stone.

COMMUTER TRAIN

I swipe through the faces,
Connections I barely touch.
Make my line, poet?

Hanging like a drying shirt
From the dowager strap.

DRUMMING IN MY EAR

My mind crumbles now.
The *shakuhachi* forgets
The late winter song.

Dismal science everywhere
Except this circle of fire.

THE AMERICAN NEWS

I choose to ignore
The American news
Whenever I can

Instead I read Lowell
To intensify my disease.

I FOLD THE PAPER

I fold the paper
Into the form of a crane,
Fictive animal...

The paper escapes its form:
The ceremony has begun.

THE GARDENER

The gardener sits on an ochre block
Of sandstone he placed in a terraced line
That stretches from beginning to end
Of all this vegetative striving.

Last year's plantings have taken hold.
Emboldened by the late spring rains,
Their silver leaves curl over the bark
That conceals the hard scratched earth

From impossible summers. The dying tree,
A dwarf eucalypt he planted twenty years
Ago, watches over the landscaped stones
And dreams his leaves green again.

Fire red kangaroo paws bloom from spears.
The old prostanthera from its pink spurs
Throws the scent of moist creek beds
All over this patch of suburban peace.

The gardener stands
To brush off his pants.

ON RENEWAL

The drinker staggered from the party,
Swore not to look above the yard arm again,
Cursed the years spent in his cups,
And found in Weimar his *neue sachlickkeit*.

The son stood outside the Moonee Ponds clinic
Where he had lured his mother into a divvy van,
Betrayed her to the psychiatric prison,
And learned the meaning of illness.

The young bureaucrat walked the streets in tears
Screamed his terrors inside his suit,
Fled the harridan on the telephone,
And climbed in ashes the mountains of his mind.

The first-time traveller in middle age
Stood and stared into the Beijing hotel yard,
Readied to leave these dreamt adventures,
And called the guide to the forbidden city.

The exile from the court lost his reason.
Cowered for weeks in his darkened room,
Where he memorised the terrible sonnets,
And composed his own song to Euridyce.

The obscure poet gathered his flowers,
Pressed them into fascicles as Emily would,
Scattered his seeds all over the feral city,
And consecrated his life to the art of ruins.

Now, the ageing historian, who hides unloved
From the hungry identities rioting at the gates,
Packs his bag for the long flight to Europe,
Prepares to abandon Thucydides' tower to the sea.

ON POWER

She tells her story
Like Zelig without humility:
Every promotion, manifest destiny;

Every failure, somebody else.
B-grade talent on a panel show,
They smile into each other's phones.

I will never sit on the interview lounge,
Lit and made up on the stage.
My helpless Anger and Scorn, sisters,

Pinion me in Peter and Paul Fortress
Where words seek out revenge
In wall-blocks of cold stone.

Sometimes, the powerless walk free from this cell
Only to stagger broken into other people as hell.

TRAVEL SONG

I stood in the library in Uppsala
Where a young, rich libertine, Foucault,
Began a beautiful lie of madness and reason
And built walls to defend against.

I circulated like Bely on Nevsky Prospekt,
Returned to Akhmatova's apartment,
Stood in Brodsky's study,
Returned from exile after death,

And stared, in an uncanny exhaustion,
At the desk where the tales
Of Alyosha and the Grand Inquisitor
Came into being.

Until at last, in the ancient capital,
Truly Europe's Third Rome,
Still haunted by Lenin's statues
And the Union of Soviet Writers,

I watched in Chisty Prud a re-enactment
Of impulsive Pushkin's romantic duel;
And in the Archangel's Cathedral imagined
A captive singer strangling my sovereign soul.

THE STATE HISTORICAL MUSEUM, MOSCOW

Strange stirrings of nothing.
Snatches of phrases
Stolen from the shaman
Who prowled the ice.

The ghosts of abandoned battles.
The mask worn by a mystic.
The copied frescoes
Of a murdered church.

In my earpiece certain monotony:
History is a determined march.
The eight decades of the Convention
Still encase the stories of this museum.

Yet in gild-frames, angels ascend,
In exquisite and pious submission,
To an unknown place
Beyond the understanding of materialists.

THE LAWS OF HISTORY

I

Not in circumstances of your own making
As if
The real was free of madness.

You never know
Whether to break the rules
Or obey tradition,

The long river that tethers
Past to present,
Blessing to catastrophe,

Where sail trade and war,
Disease and invasion,
Faith and the curse of ideas.

II

With passion and purpose
As if
Our fate lay in our hands

Our daemons were discovered
Speaking truth to power
Perched on our shoulders

Like an imprisoned angel
Who lost the power of flight
And decided to stick it out

Come what may, through thick and thin
Seeing through this choice
They did not make but must endure.

III

By stooping to drink from the slow river
As if
Anyone has time for that today

When humility has become another brand
And there are no quiet spots
Left on earth

Where the psyche can build its tower
From stone shaped by hand
In a lonely perfect circle.

Still, the clear water flows on,
While we chatter on the banks,
Onto the harbour we fear to know.

IV

Through some kind of *amor mundi*
As if
The world deserved our love

Not our critique and contempt
And constant claims for change
Our clamour for the conquest

By the last ideas
Of this frail imagined world
That will survive beyond our fall

In the flow of an inherited dream
Whose meaning we never know
Even, at the end, as we sink into its depths.

STOKER

Call me stoker
My executioners

Deny me
Even this title

Work is punishment
For living in truth

A new Stalin in an overcoat
Walks past me to buy coke zero

Her eyes locked in contempt
To avoid my existence

Imprison me in dissent
Renege on all loving debts

Reform is an excuse for cruelty
The slogan of sadists

Who want to change the country
Cleanse it of old men like me

Who know the stories they disavow
Who chant the tragic song

FOUNTAIN

I sit at the table
of Fountain House
As a guest of Akhmatova

Here the ghosts of the silver age
Speak of truer times
Forgotten youth

Here the retired physicist
Of the Soviet era conserves
The last traces of words

Here you find a seat
At the infinite conversation
But only through your own exile

Persecution, humiliation
Suffering without reward
Years of ostracism

From the bottom of that fountain
You look towards the dark sky
As the waters fill your lungs.

THE PROPHET IN A BOX

The feared red skies recede before grey rain.
The prophet sits alone, glum and empty,
In the cold steel box of his own making.

History is like that, they say -
Of your own making, not though your choosing.
But this new year, the prophet sings alone,

Knowing he has made his own prison.
Still, on the walls he scratches out
The dirges of his dark vision.

The sham impeachment breaks the republic.
The extra-judicial assassination kills the peace.
The derangement of reporting murders the truth.

All the words of all the gods
Are compressed into a zettabyte
That holds every secret and not one mystery.

Fire will destroy the forests where we camped.
Fire will destroy the beaches where we dreamt.
Fire will destroy the libraries where we survive.

Zarathustra will walk, charred and silenced,
From the stands of burning mountain ash
Into the forgotten city

There he will cry to the crowd,
What does deep midnight's voice contend?

He will shout, and wave, and drown.

But no-one is listening.
No-one can hear outside his sound-proofed box.
No-one can see the tears stain his hair shirt.

DOWN TIME

Nothing holds me against the fall,
Only little chains at my wrist,
Only fey wraps over my eyes.

The day breaks without a plan.
Play, run, muddle, read, sleep.
Make a meal then wash your bowl.

Another day I will fly to Bali;
Sing chants in a banana field;
Succumb to every forgotten pain;

But today I fall into the hole.
I slow into the darkness.
My fingers touch black vapour walls.

I twist and tumble and unknot
My ties to life before the fall.
I accelerate towards my unknown end.

In the chute, I see what I see.
Beyond my reach, I hear the beckoning words.
Beneath my time, I speak with the terrible angels.